WRITING ROMANCE

A Take-Action Workbook

Saugeen Publishers
Kitchener, Ontario

Copyright © 2019 by Heather Wright.

All rights reserved. No part of this publication may be reproduced, distributed or transmitted in any form or by any means, including photocopying, recording, or other electronic or mechanical methods, without the prior written permission of the publisher, except in the case of brief quotations embodied in critical reviews and certain other noncommercial uses permitted by copyright law. For permission requests, write to the publisher, addressed "Attention: Permissions Coordinator," at the address below.

Heather Wright
hwrightwriter@gmail.com
http://wrightingwords.com

Book Layout ©2013 BookDesignTemplates.com
Book Cover Image by Jill Wellington at Pixabay

Writing Romance: A Take-Action Workbook
Heather Wright
Saugeen Publishers
ISBN: 978-1-9991038-0-4

This book is dedicated to my husband, my son, and my mom—with enormous thanks for their unrelenting support.

You only need to look at Jane Austen to see how crossed wires can become a defining aspect of romantic life. Then again, if the course of true love ran more smoothly, it would have a terribly detrimental effect on our cache of love stories.

                    Mariella Frostrup

The sound of a kiss is not so loud as that of a cannon, but its echo lasts a great deal longer.

                    Oliver Wendell Holmes, Sr.

Contents

HOW TO USE THIS BOOK 1
CHARACTERS 5
ATTRACTION / DISTRACTION 37
PLOT PLANNERS 45
    ROMANCE IN THREE ACTS 47
    CHAPTER-BY-CHAPTER 55
SETTING 69
JOURNAL PAGES 77
CALENDAR 139
COLORING & DOODLING PAGES 164
ABOUT ME 175

v

HOW TO USE THIS BOOK

You are already doing your research, reading the fantastic books out there to help you write a great romance novel. You have ideas, notes, reflections, information. **This book is your desk-top companion on your romance-writing journey.**

Well-designed tools created especially for your genre will guide your creativity and keep you inspired. In this workbook, you can record details about your characters, your plot plans, your notes on setting, and anything else you need to regularly refer to as you create your story. This workbook also includes journal pages where you can reflect on and celebrate your work plus a calendar to track your progress.

All your notes, thoughts, questions, planning. All in one place.

Inside this book you will find worksheets, planners, and journal pages to help you develop characters, find your story, and reflect on the process. Use this book to schedule your writing time, beat writer's block with a little coloring, and best of all, get the words on the page as you've been dreaming them.

You can find out more about all my books at your online bookseller or on my website: http://www.wrightingwords.com.

If you find this book of value, **please stop by your online bookseller and leave a review**. I appreciate your time and your honest comments.

Other books in my genre-writing series--

Characters

CHARACTERS

Your favorite romance characters are memorable because their authors spent time learning what makes them tick. You want your readers to care about your characters, and the following planners will help you

Romance novels have outgrown the simple boy-girl pairings that were common in the past. People write same-gender romances, and sometimes, the love interest is a ghost or a vampire. Love can be found anywhere.

To avoid narrowing options, the romantic couple in the following pages will simply be known as Main Character 1 (MC1) and Main Character 2 (MC2). The rest is up to you.

I've added notes pages after each character planner. As you work on your novel, you will discover more interesting things about your characters, and these pages give you a place to record those inspirations.

NOTES

MC1's Name _____

Physical description	Job, hobbies, special skills
Secret that character has told no one	One thing that character is afraid of
One thing/person that character would do anything to protect	Attitude toward life, family, friends

Goals, ambitions	Experience from past that could affect relationships in the present
One virtue / one flaw	Insecurity that events in the story make worse or force character to overcome

NOTES

NOTES

MC2's Name _____

Physical description	Job, hobbies, special skills
Secret that character has told no one	One thing that character is afraid of
One thing/person that character would do anything to protect	Attitude toward life, family, friends

Goals, ambitions	Experience from past that could affect relationships in the present
One virtue / one flaw	Insecurity that events in the story make worse or force character to overcome

NOTES

NOTES

Other Character's Name _____

Physical description	Job, hobbies, special skills
Secret that character has told no one	One thing that character is afraid of
One thing/person that character would do anything to protect	Relationship to MC1 or MC2

Goals, ambitions	How this character is a helper or obstacle in the characters' relationship or in reaching their goals.
One virtue / one flaw	Opinion about either or both MCs

NOTES

NOTES

Other Character's Name _____

Physical description	Job, hobbies, special skills
Secret that character has told no one	One thing that character is afraid of
One thing/person that character would do anything to protect	Relationship to MC1 or MC2

Goals, ambitions	How this character is a helper or obstacle in the characters' relationship or in reaching their goals.
One virtue / one flaw	Opinion about either or both MCs

NOTES

NOTES

Other Character's Name _____

Physical description	Job, hobbies, special skills
Secret that character has told no one	One thing that character is afraid of
One thing/person that character would do anything to protect	Relationship to MC1 or MC2

Goals, ambitions	How this character is a helper or obstacle in the characters' relationship or in reaching their goals.
One virtue / one flaw	Opinion about either or both MCs

NOTES

NOTES

Other Character's Name _____

Physical description	Job, hobbies, special skills
Secret that character has told no one	One thing that character is afraid of
One thing/person that character would do anything to protect	Relationship to MC1 or MC2

Goals, ambitions	How this character is a helper or obstacle in the characters' relationship or in reaching their goals.
One virtue / one flaw	Opinion about either or both MCs

NOTES

NOTES

Other Character's Name _____

Physical description	Job, hobbies, special skills
Secret that character has told no one	One thing that character is afraid of
One thing/person that character would do anything to protect	Relationship to MC1 or MC2

Goals, ambitions	How this character is a helper or obstacle in the characters' relationship or in reaching their goals.
One virtue / one flaw	Opinion about either or both MCs

NOTES

NOTES

NOTES

Attraction / Distraction

ATTRACTION / DISTRACTION

The characters in your novel will certainly find each other attractive and will be considering them as potential partners. That doesn't mean that your characters have to be drop-dead gorgeous, but they should have that certain something that makes the other's heart skip a beat or two.

A romance novel is about the pull of the attraction and the push of the obstacles that distract from the romance. Use the following pages to think about the qualities in each MC that make each so appealing to the other. Then list as many problems, issues, conflicts, distractions that you can think of that could get in the way of the romance.

You might not use all of the distractions you have invented, but for now, just write down what comes into your head. No judgment. (Besides, if you don't use these ideas, they might be useful in your next novel. 😊)

Consider various sources of distractions, too, not just the character of the other MC. Nature can have a part by throwing in blizzard, or a power outage, or delayed flights, or a slip on the ice and a broken ankle. Other people put demands on your characters, too: needy friends, threatening landlords, bossy parents or siblings, police officers who don't approve of speeding …. You get the idea.

Characters overcoming obstacles are so much more interesting to read about, so give your characters plenty of trouble.

What makes MC2 so attractive to MC1 (looks, personality, perceived potential)

List the distractions that could push MC1's potential relationship or the ability to reach his/her goals off course.

What makes MC1 so attractive to MC2 (looks, personality, perceived potential)

List the distractions that could push MC2's potential relationship or the ability to reach his/her goals off course.

NOTES

NOTES

Plot Planners

PLOT PLANNERS

Romance novels are sometimes looked down upon and called formulaic. Well, guess what, romances do have a formula, and it's been around forever. The Romance Writers of America define it this way: "The main plot centers around individuals falling in love and struggling to make the relationship work ... [and who] are rewarded with emotional justice and unconditional love."
https://www.rwa.org/Online/Romance_Genre/About_Romance_Genre.aspx#The_Basics

The wonderful thing is that every writer puts their own twist on this pattern, and because of that, romance readers are blessed with innovative stories that keep them reading long after the lights should be out.

Your novel really tells two stories. One story is about the developing relationship between the two main characters. The other story follows the challenges the main character faces in trying to reach his or her goal.

I recommend creating an outline for your novel before you begin writing. Unless you have limitless time in which to write, an outline can be your friend. If you know what is going to happen next in your story, you can take advantage of short bursts of time to make progress on your novel.

If you type at 30 words per minute, you can write 450 words in 15 minutes—nearly 2 pages! An outline also ensures that you will get some writing done on those days when the muse is on sick leave or sitting, sulking in the corner and refusing to come out and play.

You can use the 3-act plan to list events that could happen in your novel, or you can break those events down even more by using the 12-chapter plot planner. Or you could use the 3-act planner to brainstorm and the 12-chapter planner to refine the order of events.

Sometimes, as you write, a brilliant plot twist will occur to you. That doesn't mean that you have to ignore it because you have a plan. You can change the plan. Writing a book rarely happens in a straight line.

You learned a lot about your characters in the previous pages. Now is the time to put that information to use as you create the plan for your romance novel.

ROMANCE IN THREE ACTS

Act 1

The two MCs meet and feel attraction. Goals and ambitions of MCs are explained. Minor characters are introduced. Source of conflict between two MCs is revealed. Doubts arise that conflict could ever be overcome.

ACT 2

Most of the action of the story happens here. Moments when the relationship seems possible are followed by events that seem to push the characters further apart.

ACT 3

This act begins with a final obstacle that seems insurmountable. Finally, the MCs overcome this obstacle and their growing love for each other is revealed and celebrated.

CHAPTER-BY-CHAPTER

Chapters 1 and 2

Introduction of main characters and their goals in the story. These chapters should include their first meeting, attraction, goals, initial conflict, and the setting in which story takes place.

Chapters 3 through 6

Further development of conflict with this section escalating to Chapter 7. Continuation of the steps MC1 is taking to reach his/her goal and dealing with problems and people encountered along the way

Chapter 7

This chapter culminates in a conflict that seems too big to ever be resolved.

Chapters 8 through 10

Low point for relationship. Determination to put all efforts into reaching goal.

Chapter 11

MC overcomes most challenging moment in relationship and in quest for goal.

Chapter 12

Resolution, happy ending, plans for future.

NOTES

Setting

SETTING

Even if you are writing about your home town, you are going to have to do some research. Use the next few pages to record what you do know, list the questions you need to research, write down any resources, or draw any maps that you may need for reference.

Some series romance novels are set in a particular area or even on a particular street. If you plan to take that approach, knowing exactly where people live, shop and play, and who they meet every day will be important because your characters will be visiting the same neighbourhood again and again.

If you are writing an historical romance, you have an even greater challenge. Aside from getting their clothing and the details of the setting right, you also need to watch your characters' diction. A great resource for finding out if a particular word existed during your story's time period is *English Through the Ages* by William Brohaugh.

When you are writing about the past or about the distant future, consider the following topics when you are doing the research to create your story's world:

- Government/ruling class
- Money/how the economy works
- Religious class and power
- Geography
- Climate

- Clothing and how produced/purchased
- Food/diet
- Transportation
- Methods of communication
- Housing
- Science
- School/training
- Medicine

NOTES

NOTES

NOTES

Maps and Drawings

Maps and Drawings

Journal Pages

JOURNAL PAGES

Here are 30 days of journal pages for you to record your progress through this book and through drafting your novel. You don't have to write a journal entry every day. Maybe once a week will keep you on track towards your target.

Completing these pages will help you reflect on your process, determine next steps, and record any shiny, do-not-belong-in-this-novel ideas that come to you while you're working on your current project.

When things get tough, or if you feel you are blocked, it's easy to want to drop what you are doing and go with the next shiny thing in your mind. I encourage you to capture these shiny ideas but leave them for later.

Yes, there are writing days when you will feel like you're trying to run uphill in two feet of mud, but those feelings are also part of the writer's life. Every writer faces them—and you are a writer. You can overcome those challenges and reach your goal.

Finishing is your best reward.

Date _____

The Step I Took Toward My Goal

_____

_____

_____

_____

_____

_____

My Surprises, Inspirations, Shiny Things

_____

_____

_____

_____

_____

_____

My Next Steps

To Do (research, word count goals, reading the experts ....)

Date _____

The Step I Took Toward My Goal

My Surprises, Inspirations, Shiny Things

My Next Steps

_____
_____
_____
_____
_____
_____

To Do (research, word count goals, reading the experts ....)

- _____
- _____
- _____
- _____
- _____
- _____

Date _____

The Step I Took Toward My Goal

_____
_____
_____
_____
_____
_____

My Surprises, Inspirations, Shiny Things

_____
_____
_____
_____
_____
_____

My Next Steps

To Do (research, word count goals, reading the experts ….)

Date _____

The Step I Took Toward My Goal

My Surprises, Inspirations, Shiny Things

My Next Steps

To Do (research, word count goals, reading the experts ....)

Date _____

The Step I Took Toward My Goal

My Surprises, Inspirations, Shiny Things

My Next Steps

To Do (research, word count goals, reading the experts ....)

Date _____

The Step I Took Toward My Goal

My Surprises, Inspirations, Shiny Things

My Next Steps

To Do (research, word count goals, reading the experts ....)

Date _____

The Step I Took Toward My Goal

_____
_____
_____
_____
_____
_____

My Surprises, Inspirations, Shiny Things

_____
_____
_____
_____
_____
_____

My Next Steps

To Do (research, word count goals, reading the experts ….)

Date _____

The Step I Took Toward My Goal

My Surprises, Inspirations, Shiny Things

My Next Steps

To Do (research, word count goals, reading the experts ....)

Date _____

The Step I Took Toward My Goal

_____
_____
_____
_____
_____
_____

My Surprises, Inspirations, Shiny Things

_____
_____
_____
_____
_____
_____

My Next Steps

To Do (research, word count goals, reading the experts ....)

Date _____

The Step I Took Toward My Goal

_____
_____
_____
_____
_____
_____

My Surprises, Inspirations, Shiny Things

_____
_____
_____
_____
_____
_____

My Next Steps

To Do (research, word count goals, reading the experts ....)

Date _____

The Step I Took Toward My Goal

_____

_____

_____

_____

_____

_____

My Surprises, Inspirations, Shiny Things

_____

_____

_____

_____

_____

_____

My Next Steps

To Do (research, word count goals, reading the experts ....)

Date _____

The Step I Took Toward My Goal

_____

_____

_____

_____

_____

_____

My Surprises, Inspirations, Shiny Things

_____

_____

_____

_____

_____

_____

My Next Steps

To Do (research, word count goals, reading the experts ....)

Date _____

The Step I Took Toward My Goal

_____
_____
_____
_____
_____
_____

My Surprises, Inspirations, Shiny Things

_____
_____
_____
_____
_____
_____

My Next Steps

To Do (research, word count goals, reading the experts ….)

Date _____

The Step I Took Toward My Goal

_____
_____
_____
_____
_____
_____

My Surprises, Inspirations, Shiny Things

_____
_____
_____
_____
_____
_____

My Next Steps

To Do (research, word count goals, reading the experts ....)

Date _____

The Step I Took Toward My Goal

My Surprises, Inspirations, Shiny Things

My Next Steps

To Do (research, word count goals, reading the experts ….)

Date _____

The Step I Took Toward My Goal

My Surprises, Inspirations, Shiny Things

My Next Steps

To Do (research, word count goals, reading the experts ….)

Date _____

The Step I Took Toward My Goal

_____
_____
_____
_____
_____
_____

My Surprises, Inspirations, Shiny Things

_____
_____
_____
_____
_____
_____

My Next Steps

To Do (research, word count goals, reading the experts ….)

Date _____

The Step I Took Toward My Goal

My Surprises, Inspirations, Shiny Things

My Next Steps

To Do (research, word count goals, reading the experts ....)

Date _____

The Step I Took Toward My Goal

My Surprises, Inspirations, Shiny Things

My Next Steps

_____
_____
_____
_____
_____
_____

To Do (research, word count goals, reading the experts ....)

- _____
- _____
- _____
- _____
- _____
- _____

Date _____

The Step I Took Toward My Goal

_____
_____
_____
_____
_____
_____

My Surprises, Inspirations, Shiny Things

_____
_____
_____
_____
_____
_____

My Next Steps

To Do (research, word count goals, reading the experts ….)

Date _____

The Step I Took Toward My Goal

_____
_____
_____
_____
_____
_____

My Surprises, Inspirations, Shiny Things

_____
_____
_____
_____
_____
_____

My Next Steps

To Do (research, word count goals, reading the experts ….)

Date _____

The Step I Took Toward My Goal

_____
_____
_____
_____
_____
_____

My Surprises, Inspirations, Shiny Things

_____
_____
_____
_____
_____
_____

My Next Steps

To Do (research, word count goals, reading the experts ....)

Date _____

The Step I Took Toward My Goal

My Surprises, Inspirations, Shiny Things

My Next Steps

To Do (research, word count goals, reading the experts ....)

Date _____

The Step I Took Toward My Goal

My Surprises, Inspirations, Shiny Things

My Next Steps

To Do (research, word count goals, reading the experts ....)

Date _____

The Step I Took Toward My Goal

My Surprises, Inspirations, Shiny Things

My Next Steps

To Do (research, word count goals, reading the experts ....)

Date _____

The Step I Took Toward My Goal

_____
_____
_____
_____
_____
_____

My Surprises, Inspirations, Shiny Things

_____
_____
_____
_____
_____
_____

My Next Steps

To Do (research, word count goals, reading the experts ....)

Date _____

The Step I Took Toward My Goal

_____

_____

_____

_____

_____

_____

My Surprises, Inspirations, Shiny Things

_____

_____

_____

_____

_____

_____

My Next Steps

To Do (research, word count goals, reading the experts ....)

Date _____

The Step I Took Toward My Goal

My Surprises, Inspirations, Shiny Things

My Next Steps

To Do (research, word count goals, reading the experts ....)

Date _____

The Step I Took Toward My Goal

My Surprises, Inspirations, Shiny Things

My Next Steps

To Do (research, word count goals, reading the experts ....)

Date _____

The Step I Took Toward My Goal

_____

_____

_____

_____

_____

My Surprises, Inspirations, Shiny Things

_____

_____

_____

_____

_____

My Next Steps

To Do (research, word count goals, reading the experts ....)

Calendar

CALENDAR

It can take a long time to write a book, so I've included a full year of blank calendars for you to use to track your progress. Since this book contains a collection of your thoughts and plans, it's a good place to record your word count or time spent writing or whatever you choose to log to keep you inspired by your progress.

Remember, writing in small pieces works, and you have the advantage of having spent time outlining your story. You don't have to wait for the muse to drop by; you know what you are working on next. And you can write out of order, too, if you like. If one scene is really clear in your mind, write it, and put it where it belongs later.

Consider the numbers. If you write 250 words (1 page double-spaced) for 300 days a year you will have 75,000 words. Even if you only type at 30 words a minute, 250 words takes less than 10 minutes a day. I find these numbers encouraging—and they also take away the excuse that I don't have enough time to write.

NOTES

Month _____

Sun	Mon	Tues	Wed	Thurs	Fri	Sat

NOTES

Month _____

Sun	Mon	Tues	Wed	Thurs	Fri	Sat

NOTES

Month _____

Sun	Mon	Tues	Wed	Thurs	Fri	Sat

NOTES

Month _____

Sun	Mon	Tues	Wed	Thurs	Fri	Sat

NOTES

Month _____

Sun	Mon	Tues	Wed	Thurs	Fri	Sat

NOTES

Month _____

Sun	Mon	Tues	Wed	Thurs	Fri	Sat

NOTES

Month _____

Sun	Mon	Tues	Wed	Thurs	Fri	Sat

NOTES

Month _____

Sun	Mon	Tues	Wed	Thurs	Fri	Sat

NOTES

Month _____

Sun	Mon	Tues	Wed	Thurs	Fri	Sat

NOTES

Month _____

Sun	Mon	Tues	Wed	Thurs	Fri	Sat

NOTES

Month _____

Sun	Mon	Tues	Wed	Thurs	Fri	Sat

NOTES

Month _____

Sun	Mon	Tues	Wed	Thurs	Fri	Sat

Coloring & Doodling Pages

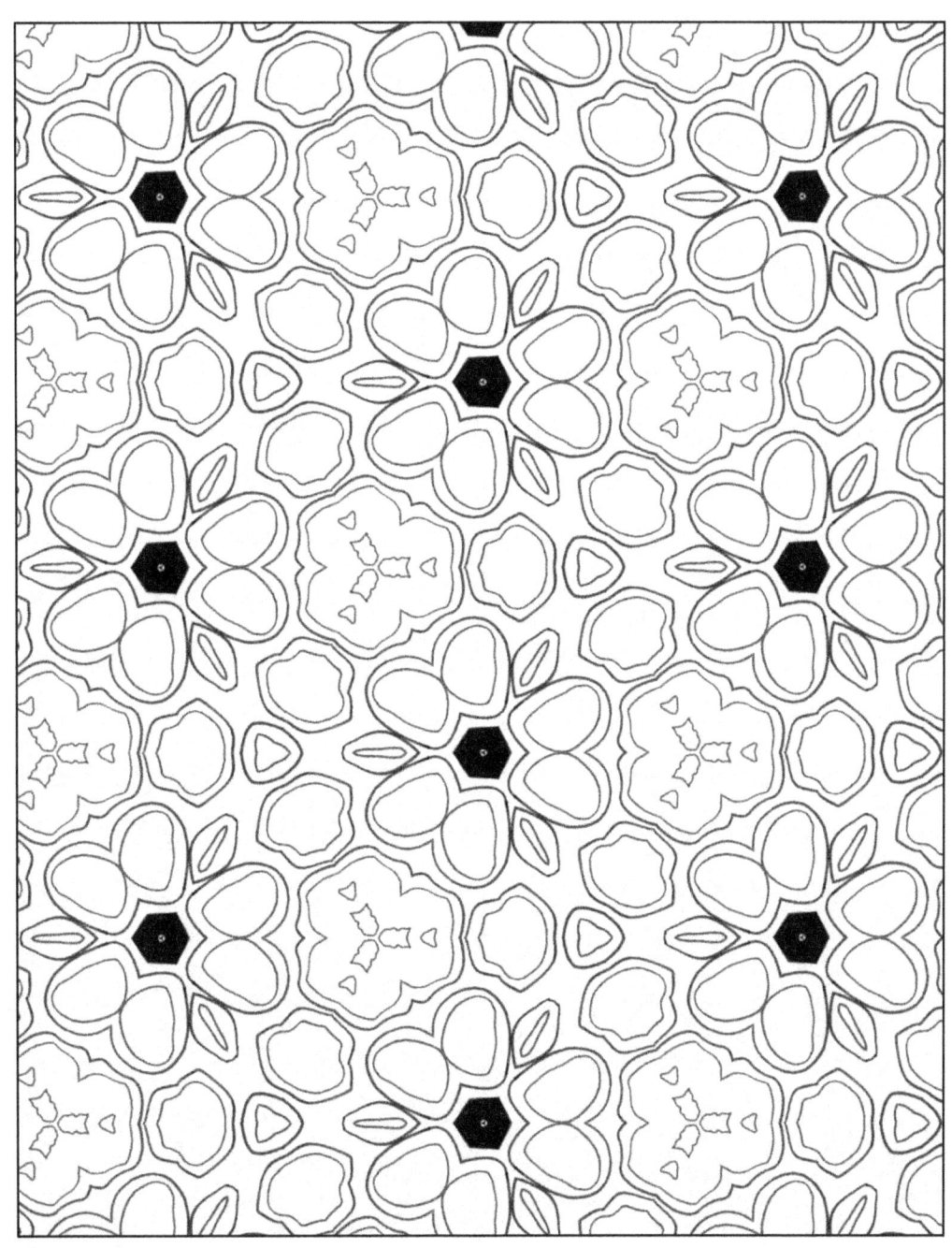

Image by KaylinArt on Pixabay

Image by Alexandra Zeres from Pixabay

Image by Kaylin Art from Pixabay

Image by KaylinArt on Pixabay

ABOUT ME

I always have more than one work-in-progress. I own too many journals, and I love red licorice, buttered popcorn, and chocolate–not together. I'm grateful for coffee shops where I can go to kickstart stalled projects. I love music, old films, and sing soprano in a choir. (Secret: I leave the really high notes for those who can land them without a squeak.)

I can't imagine my life without writers, watching them become motivated and empowered, and reading the great work that they create. As a coach, I love working one-on-one with writers of all ages. My current clients range in age from 15 to 90.

I am also a freelance writer, writing about everything from orchids to wind turbines to weddings to PVC pipe. I have written for national and local publications, and for educational publishers and industry.

My website, **http://www.wrightingwords.com**, hosts my blog and offers links to all my books for writers. You'll also find lots of free resources for writers of all ages and their teachers, too.

If you found this book of value, **please stop by your online bookseller and leave a review**. I appreciate your time and your honest comments.

www.ingramcontent.com/pod-product-compliance
Lightning Source LLC
Chambersburg PA
CBHW081357070526
44583CB00020B/2581